Praise for Work Yourself Happy

"With polls showing that half of all Americans would change careers if given the chance, Terri Levine's message could not be arriving at a better time. Work Yourself Happy is the mission of our times."

Laura Berman Fortgang, author, *Take Yourself to the Top; The Secrets of America's #1 Career Coach*

"Work Yourself Happy is full of practical tips and useful exercises designed to keep your attitude and dreams on track. It's a first aid kit for the ailing career."

Marcia Reynolds, author, Capture the Rapture. Past president, International Coach Federation

"Don't be fooled by its size. Work Yourself Happy is a small primer with a big message. A must gift for yourself. Coaching at its best!"

Bonnie Ross-Parker, Associate Publisher, The Gazette Newspaper

"You have compiled and organized many of the secrets of success. I believe a person will find themselves and find happiness if they follow your guide."

Robert A. O'Hare, president, Performance Improvement

"Truly joyful people enjoy their work as much as their leisure time, and author Terri Levine offers simple strategies and guidelines for how to become engaged in your work in a joyful way."

Azriela Jaffe, author, Create Your Own Luck

"This is a real value. In this simple book lies the most powerful guide to creating happiness, while achieving success, I have ever seen. And, you can rest assured, Terri's wisdom works; her phenomenal success and happiness is the proof."

BETH MEININGER, PASSION FOR LIFE COACH

"A great self-help book which generates many 'ah-ha' moments. From the exercises and case studies to Terri Levine's wise and pragmatic advice, this book guides you to greater self-awareness and appreciation. It got me excited about taking charge of my work and my life."

LESLIE WYATT, RN,MS, ADMINISTRATOR, CHILDREN'S HOSPITAL, RICHMOND,VA

"Terri Levine has captured the essence of, 'Take time to take time.' A must read for most of us who complain we don't have time to take care of ourselves. Her ideas are both practical and fun to experience."

BILL THOMAS, MA, MCC, PRESIDENT, COACH SQUARED

"Perfect if you want balance *and* happiness in your work life."

MARILEE GOLDBERG ADAMS, PH.D., AUTHOR, *THE ART OF THE QUESTION*

"Work Yourself Happy gives practical tips to fulfillment and enjoyment in your work and life."

NANCY BAKER, COFOUNDER PHILADELPHIA AREA COACHES ALLIANCE

WORK
YOURSELF
HAPPY™

A Step-by-Step Guide To Creating
Joy In Your Life And Work

By Terri Levine

Published by:
LAHASKA PRESS
PO BOX 1147
BUCKINGHAM, PA 18912

ISBN: 0-9650534–3–1

Publisher's Cataloging-in-Publication

Levine, Terri.

Work yourself happy: a step by step guide to creating joy in your
life and work / by Terri Levine. --

1st ed.

P.CM

ISBN: 0-9650534-3-1

1. Job satisfaction 2. Career development.

3. Stress management I. TITLE

HF5549.5.J63L48 2000   650.1

QB100-766

Printed in the United States of America

ACKNOWLEDGEMENTS

I dedicate this book to my loving husband, Mark, who is my partner in friendship and love and the reason for my happiness. He is my best friend, my lover, my soul-mate, my husband. He always gives me his inspiration to be myself and do what makes me happy. I love you completely and am thankful you love me the same way.

My mother, Helen, resting in peace. She was my first love. She was my confidante, best friend, and mentor. She taught me to make myself happy and to do what I love.

My father, Walter, who gave me many gifts of public speaking, selling skills, and self-confidence.

My sister, Lynn, who told me to "go for it" and believed I'd be successful no matter what I did.

My friends, Beth Swetits and Elaine Dial who told me to honor my true passion and believed in me.

Sharon Teitelbaum, for her gift in coaching me with patience, respect, care, and giving me a way to get in touch with my own voice and to live my own dreams.

Jim Donovan, for his wisdom, patience, editing talent, and his wonderful advice, encouragement and belief in Work Yourself Happy!

Stephanie Lisle, an extraordinary photographer who made a photo shoot fun, and relaxing.

Lynn Ann Donchez, an amazing artist who worked wonders with hair and make-up in a flash.

TABLE OF CONTENTS

FOREWORD

How many people do you know who are truly happy in their work? Are you? When you consider the amount of time we spend commuting to and from work, working or talking about work with friends and co-workers, it stands to reason we would want to be happy doing whatever it is we do for eight, ten or twelve hours a day.

Unfortunately, the sad truth is that most people are not happy in their jobs. Most people celebrate Fridays (TGIF) and dread Monday mornings. As a matter of fact, according to Dr. Bernie Segal, a very high percentage of people who die from heart attacks do so on Monday mornings. Their dislike for their work is so intense it brings about their demise.

Terri Levine was on a fast track to become one of those people when something in her changed. She decided she was no longer willing to live this way. She had the courage to change and found she could, in fact, be both happy and successful. In *Work Yourself Happy*, she shares her insights, experiences, fears and successes as a road map for the rest of us who want to be happy in our working lives.

As a successful coach, Terri has a unique gift, being able to guide each of us toward what we want and need in order to be happy in our working lives. For some, it may mean finding a new career. For others, simply changing parts of your current job. Some of you may want to stop work altogether and start your own business. Whatever your situation, *Work Yourself Happy* will help you uncover your deepest desires, help you tap into the courage you'll need to face your fears and provide you with ideas and techniques you can use to begin creating a life you'll love. You deserve no less. Happiness is your birthright.

Having been one of the fortunate people who has found work I love, I am honored to have been a part of producing this book.

I know Terri Levine and I know how much she has to offer you, the reader. She is living proof that you *can* work yourself happy.

If you want to find happiness in your work, you are holding in your hand right now a guide that will help you achieve your desires. It's now up to you.

JIM DONOVAN
Author, Handbook To A Happier Life

"

had a dream that I could re-invent my career and design a life that works. It was a dream that became my vision.

Nothing happens without first a dream.

"

TERRI LEVINE

Work Yourself Happy

"It is not God's will merely that we should be happy, but that we should make ourselves happy."

IMMANUEL KANT

What does *Work Yourself Happy* mean? Does it mean denying your needs and working so hard that you lose yourself in your career? Of course not. Does it mean accepting whatever job you happen to have and learning to "grin and bear it?" Not likely. Does it mean working in a job you hate but telling yourself you're enjoying it? Emphatically no!

Working yourself happy is coming to the realization that success does not mean job burn-out, unhealthy stress, being away from the things and people you love, not having time for yourself and your needs, and not being passionate about your work.

It means deciding that you will no longer tolerate a life that doesn't include work that fully nurtures you. It means that you perform incredibly at work because you enjoy it so much. It means you work less and accomplish more. It means you have a career you love and work you are passionate about.

I am deeply saddened when I meet people who are stuck in a career, company or profession that does not feed their soul every day. Is this what life has to offer? I know that there is more because I was once caught up in having the right degrees, the high level jobs and the big income. I had all the trappings of what we were taught was "success." Only, I was miserable! I didn't sleep, I ate poorly and had no time for exercise, friends, family or hobbies. I worked late and was never able to stop thinking about my job. When I was at home, I was on e-mail at midnight. I checked voice mail constantly on my vacation. I was not controlling my life or my job. I was in a rut, trapped by the trappings of so-called success.

MY STORY

I am fortunate because I decided that I was no longer willing to allow money, prestige, and the "gee, I ought to's" to control me. It took a lot of courage and I had to face my greatest fears; however, it also led to my making major life-changing decisions.

With the help and support of my personal coach, I was able to recognize that my passion and zest for living were dead. I learned that my life was being eaten up by work, my relationships were suffering, and my health and well-being were in serious jeopardy. One day, this struck me like a bolt of lightning. When I finally saw it, I knew I had to put my fears aside and take action — now! Otherwise, my time here on earth would be about a job I didn't want instead of the life that I had the choice - yes the choice - to design and to live.

My real passion, which I am now following, is helping

people like you create and live the lives you dream of. I'm here as a reminder that you have the freedom to make choices and to encourage you to take the first step in admitting to yourself that you are not doing what you love to do. To begin this change, you must first recognize that the unknown can be very scary, but the benefits of change can bring you freedom beyond your wildest imagination and a life that will make you want to jump out of bed each day with joy and excitement. You deserve nothing less.

If you aren't singing and playing and laughing out loud, then I encourage you to uncover your passion. Read each chapter in this book and complete the exercises. Come along with me on this fabulous and delightful journey called life.

I am so delighted to share this with you because the lesson that I learned is so great and so meaningful to me and it's so simple — allow yourself to be you and work yourself happy. Life is not about being suppressed or accepting less than you deserve.

THIS BOOK'S FOR YOU IF:

You want to make a career change.

You want to change jobs.

You want to move up and get a promotion.

You want to restructure your job.

You want assistance job hunting.

You want to understand how to have a job you enjoy.

You want to improve your skills on the job.

You want to increase what you are paid.

You want to improve relations with your employees or employer or co-workers.

You want assistance in preparing for interviews.

You want to learn how to do your job with less effort.

You want to learn how to leave the office behind — really leave it, so you can go home and enjoy life.

You are ready to be an entrepreneur.

You want to re-invent or re-define your job description.

What does this all mean? To me,
it is one thing — it is the concept of:

ACCEPTANCE

HOW TO BEST READ THIS BOOK

As a suggestion, you may want to read the entire book first. Then, come back and re-read the book, highlighting the parts that touch you and ignite your passion. Then, complete each of the exercises to the best of your ability. Make doing them an enjoyable process. After all, this book is about working yourself happy.

I recommend you use a journal to record the answers to the exercises as well as your thoughts and feelings, dreams and plans. This is something you will want to come back to later, as you progress in your life. It's great to have a reference point to show you just how far you've come in your growth.

THE FIVE SECRETS TO WORKING YOURSELF HAPPY

SECRET 1: ACCEPT THAT YOU MUST LET GO OF THE PAST.

SECRET 2: TAKE A CLOSE LOOK AT YOUR PREVIOUS ENDEAVORS.

SECRET 3: GET TO KNOW YOURSELF REALLY WELL.

SECRET 4: CREATE A DESTINATION WITH SOUL.

SECRET 5: ENJOY THE JOURNEY.

Now, let's explore each of these in greater detail.

ACCEPTANCE

How many times have you heard someone say, "Losing my job was the best thing that ever happened to me"? Does hearing this sentiment make you scratch your head in puzzlement? How could something so negative be so positive? What's the person's secret?

Few of us begin our careers with the intent of doing something else. After all, we've invested quite a bit of time and money getting to where we are.

We spend thousands of dollars and several years of our lives in pursuit of our degrees. We then invest even more time going after postgraduate degrees. An attorney, for example, spends a total of nineteen years in the pursuit of a law degree and then has to pass an extremely difficult exam, one which many fail on their first attempt.

Doctors spend even more time in school and then devote even more years to internship and residency programs. Sadly, many of these dedicated professionals then find out they are not happy in their chosen work. Much like Humpty Dumpty, we proudly sit atop our wall of achievements and accomplishments, giving little thought to doing anything else.

"After all, I worked hard to get where I am and I'm proud of it. I'm good at what I do and people respect me. You can't expect me to want to give all this up, can you?" These are the words you hear from your logical, rational mind (or friends and family) whenever you even think about making a career change. Unfortunately, your true self, that part of you who knows what's in your best interest, is often screaming for a change, nagging away at your thoughts until you begin to listen.

Even if you're content in your present job, with today's changing workplace and the uncertainty in the corporate world, it's likely that sooner or later in your working life, you will find yourself, much like our friend Humpty, tumbling from the security of your little perch.

For most of us the great fall occurs when one or more of the following occurs:

• Our job is eliminated through downsizing.

• Our company is acquired or merges with another company and the new situation no longer appeals to us.

• Our job stays the same but we just can't get excited about it anymore.

So, after the great fall what are the secrets to putting yourself back together again — better and happier than ever?

SECRET 1: ACCEPT THAT YOU MUST LET GO OF THE PAST

"Progress is a nice word. But change is its motivator.
And change has its enemies."

ROBERT KENNEDY

*B*y its very definition, change begins with an ending. Acknowledge the loss and your feelings associated with it. Realize that it is perfectly normal to feel sadness and some confusion. Seek support from friends, family members, a therapist or a personal coach. Work through these feelings. Don't deny or ignore them.

CHANGE

For centuries, people believed that Aristotle was right when he said that the heavier an object, the faster it would fall to earth. Aristotle was regarded as the greatest thinker of all time and surely he could not be wrong. All it would have taken was for one brave person to take two objects, one heavy and one light, and drop them from a great height to see whether or not the heavier object landed first. But no one stepped forward until nearly 2,000 years after Aristotle's death. In 1589, Galileo summoned learned professors to the base of the Leaning Tower of Pisa. Then he went to the top and pushed off a ten-pound and a one-pound weight. Both landed at the same time. But the power of belief in the conventional wisdom was so strong that the professors denied what they had seen.

They continued to say Aristotle was right, reinforcing the observation made by Niccolo Machiavelli in his book *The Prince*. He wrote that, "There is nothing more difficult to take in hand, more perilous to conduct, or more uncertain in its success than to take the lead in the introduction of a new order of things."

Change is inevitable. Everything in the Universe is constantly changing, right down to the very cells in your body. Change is going to happen, with or without your permission. You might as well learn to accept change, since it's happening anyway. As a matter of fact, if you can learn to welcome change and develop a belief that "change is good," you will be much happier and better able to handle whatever life sends your way.

TURNING ANXIETY INTO OPPORTUNITY

Why do some people blossom in the face of stress while others wither? The determining factor may be how much you feel in control of your life. People who choose their paths, regardless of how stressful they are, don't suffer from stress as much as those who have no choice. As a matter of fact, mental health professionals confirm that a good measure of your mental health is the amount of control you feel you have over your own life. The more you feel in control of your life and destiny, the healthier you are mentally.

TAKE CONTROL

How can you take control of your life? The first step is to get organized. Figure out what's important, then do it. Learn not to waste time on little things that don't matter. Many people put off organization because it takes time and energy at first, but the benefits of being in control of your time and energy outweigh the initial investment.

Taking care of yourself also puts you in control. Be deliberate about what you eat. Choose foods that are high in energy-producing complex carbohydrates and low in fat and sugar. Translation: Avoid junk food. Get energy from fresh fruits and vegetables, natural snacks and sandwiches that are light on mayonnaise and other fatty dressings. Skip the cocktail or extra cup of coffee. Caffeine and alcohol make stress worse. Set aside some time every day for your own mental and physical health. Exercise, relaxation activities and fun all enhance your sense of being in control of your life. We will explore these ideas in greater detail later in this book.

"Change and growth take place when a person has risked himself
and dares to experiment with his own life."

HERBERT OTTO

BE OPEN TO CHANGE

All of us are subject to the curves life throws at us. There are two ways to react to change. You can let it buffet you about like a strong wind or you can use it to fill your sails and help you get where you want to go. Ironically, you increase your sense of control when you're open to change. Look at each change as an opportunity to gain new skills and knowledge. Not sure you like your new boss? Find out what makes your boss tick and what changes you can make so you're more valuable to your boss and your company.

Control and openness to change are the keys to turning anxiety into opportunity. You can't always choose your destiny in life, but you can choose how to cope with it. The more you're "in the driver's seat," the easier it will be to cope with stress.

TEN WAYS TO COPE WITH THE CHANGE

In these days of downsizing, many of us are asked to be more productive and carry a larger workload, often causing us to feel overwhelmed and frustrated. As we begin to feel overwhelmed, it becomes even more difficult to deal with problems and cope with feelings that all this change is triggering.

Incorporate one or two or more of the strategies below to help yourself deal with the changes you are experiencing. They have worked for many of us. See which ones work best for you.

1. Allow yourself to feel empowered. If you feel and act like a victim, you will not be able to help yourself. No one is going to save you from the situation at work and only you have the power and responsibility to change it. So stop complaining and stand up and prepare yourself for change.

2. Be fully present. Focus on each task you are dealing with rather than where you have to be next or how much paperwork you need to finish. If you put all of your energy into the here and now, you will get more accomplished and feel less frustrated.

3. Examine all your duties and see what is not mandatory. At first glance, you'll probably think they are all mandatory. Look again. Which ones can be simplified, delegated, or done in less time without compromising the outcome? List all of your duties and you will begin to see what is not required.

4. Take some breaks. Stretch or get some water, or take a walk several times a day. During lunch, find a way to rest your mind. Give yourself the mental break you need. Read or listen to music or talk to friends to escape work and feel more peaceful.

5. Close the door and go home. At the end of the day, close the door and leave all of your work problems behind the door. You may even visualize a box that you are putting a lid on and it cannot be reopened until the next day. Say good-bye to your workplace each evening.

6. Allow yourself time and space to get your feelings out. Try writing in a journal to say what you are feeling about your job situation. Express all your anger and sadness in your journal.

7. Maintain open communication with family and friends. Share your feelings out loud and seek the advice and support of your family, close friends, a career counselor or support group. Listen to what your support systems are saying and be open to new ideas.

8. Stay motivated. Take hot baths, listen to soothing music, exercise, eat healthy and enjoy the company of friends. Have some solitude each day. Come up with a list of 20 things that will really bring you joy and pleasure every day. Whenever you really feel stressed, take out the list and make time in the day to do things that will reduce your stress.

9. Remember that work is often cyclical. The fact that you have more work this week than ever before doesn't mean it will be this way next week. Remember it will change and your workload will shift again.

10. If you find yourself unable to make the situation any better, focus on the positive. If you choose to stay in your current job, decide why you are staying. There must be some positives: the people you work with, the benefits, the distance from your home. Focus on those and refuse to engage in negative chatter with your co-workers. Pull yourself up rather than down. It is a choice you can make.

TOXIC PEOPLE

We've all seen them. People who, when you are in their presence, drain your energy. Jack Canfield, co-author of the *Chicken Soup for the Soul* series, calls them "Energy vampires."

These are the people who, no matter what, choose to focus on the negative in any situation. They're always finding fault with the company, their co-workers or whatever is going on in their lives. They will drag you down, even if you're having a great day. These are the people who never have anything good to say about anyone or anything, themselves included. They are the people who, without being asked, will tell you why your great idea for a new business venture will never work and why you'll wind up just losing all your money. They'll tell you why you are not qualified for a promotion and what's wrong with your boss. They usually spend a lot of time engaged in gossip and are rarely happy.

While you may be saddened seeing people living their

lives at such a low level of enjoyment, for your own well-being, avoid them at all cost. Minimize your interaction with these people or they will surely suck the energy and enthusiasm from you.

SECRET 2: TAKE A CLOSE LOOK AT YOUR PREVIOUS ENDEAVORS

*C*onsider each of your previous jobs as a "test-drive." What are the lessons that can be learned? What aspects did you enjoy? What things did you tolerate? What made your blood boil? What energized you? What were you most proud of accomplishing? As you work on the exercises that follow, look for common threads that appear.

JENNIFER'S STORY

Jennifer, a successful attorney, was part of a large law firm. She became sick and tired of the hassles of law, the long hours, and the fact that the legal system is based on fighting and arguing. She also found herself unable to fit into what she felt was a male-dominated profession.

She had no idea what to do next and came to me as a coaching client to help her see new opportunities. In our sessions, I had her go back to the things she loved but never had time to do. Things like taking walks, eating three meals a day, seeing friends, playing with her cat, buying herself flowers, listening to music, and just being.

After a while, she decided what she really wanted was to work at a job that was less stressful, one that would allow her to enjoy her life more. She was no longer willing to let money drive her life. She found a part-time job in a coffee shop and another in a bookstore. She doesn't miss working in law and, since both new jobs nourish her soul, she is enjoying her new life more than ever.

LOOKING BACK EXERCISE

Sit somewhere quiet, where you will not be interrupted for a while and let your mind drift back to your childhood. What did you enjoy doing at age six or seven? What were the activities that gave you pleasure? What about your teen years and early adulthood? What did you enjoy then? What were some of your first jobs? What kinds of activities did they include?

In your journal or workbook, begin making notes about these different activities, especially jobs you really liked. Go all the way back to when you were a youngster, perhaps working at a part-time job while still in high school. What were some of the things you did? Be sure to include volunteer projects and community work.

For example, one woman I know, after completing this exercise, discovered that one of her favorite jobs was when she worked as a babysitter throughout high school. Today she is the owner of a nanny service that provides infant and childcare services to working couples.

Another woman decided, after a distinguished career in high technology, to choose early retirement. She then went back to an earlier calling she had experienced for a short time right after college. She had always wanted to work in the theatre and had forsaken it to pursue a "better paying" job. Today she works part-time in a regional theatre company and loves it.

Next to each job on your list, make some notes about how you felt about the job at the time. In her classic small business book, *Working Solo*, author Terri Lonier informs us of a study conducted by British behavioral scientists, on the relationship between our desires in youth and adult success.

Fifty individuals were tracked over a period of 28 years, from the age of seven to 35. The result was nearly all of the subjects wound up engaged in a professional pursuit related to their interests during the ages seven through 14. While most strayed from these interests after childhood, the successful adults were those who found their way back to their childhood dreams by the age of 35, even if only as a hobby or avocation.

What about your adult career? What does that list look like? Next to each of your past jobs, make a brief note as to how you felt about the work, people, company, etc. What parts of the job made you happy? What parts did you dislike? Are there some similar traits that keep popping up? Maybe all the jobs you had involved working with small children, as in our babysitter example. Perhaps you notice a lot of your past work experience is working with the public or machinery. Look for patterns here.

"Nothing is work unless you'd rather be doing something else"
JACK RETTIG

WHAT ARE YOUR INTERESTS?

Work doesn't have to be negative or unpleasant. It has often been said that the ultimate goal of career planning is to find something you enjoy doing and then find someone who will pay you to do it.

It is important not to underestimate the role of interests in your career plan. The more closely your day-to-day work matches your interests, the more likely it is that you will be happy doing it. It's a pretty simple concept. If you loathe being in the outdoors, you'll probably not be happy working as a Park Ranger. Likewise, if the idea of sitting at a computer terminal all day turns you off, then being a web designer will not be your best choice as a career. Granted, it may be financially rewarding, especially in today's technology marketplace, however, the lure of the money can wear off quickly as you realize you're spending a good portion of your life doing something you dislike. As my friend Jim Donovan says, "This is your life, not a dress rehearsal."

Most jobs fit into one or more categories such as Manual/Practical –working with your hands, Trades/Crafts –working with things, Scientific/Technical –working with ideas and intellect, Creative –work requiring self-expression, Social –helping people, Business –working with people,

Information Management –working with data and details. The following exercise may help you to identify your interests.

INTERESTS EXERCISE

In order to develop your personal profile, think about what you enjoy doing. What kinds of day-to-day activities appeal to you? Would you be happy spending your days talking to groups of people or would you rather be making or repairing something, using your hands?

Does the idea of creating with a computer excite you or are you more interested in being out in the fresh air? Do you like dealing with small children? Do you like meeting new people? How about taking care of the elderly; Does that sound like something you would enjoy? Maybe you've always wanted to own your own business. If so, doing what?

In your journal, write the kinds of activities you feel you would enjoy doing on a daily basis. Once you have determined your interests, you'll want to explore some of the other areas of your personality in order to paint a clear picture of what will make you the happiest. Remember the goal is to work in a job that makes you happy. Not one in which you simply *"get by."*

In your journal, answer the following:

What are your needs? What kinds of experiences do you need in order to be happy and feel fulfilled? Is challenge important to you? What about security, opportunity, income level and so on. We will explore your values in more detail later in this book but, for now, answer these questions as best as you can.

What are your abilities?

What do you naturally do well?

What are your aptitudes?

What do you learn easily?

What level of physical activity is acceptable to you?

To help answer these questions, think back to your previous jobs. What are some of the things you liked about them? What were their strong points?

YOUR PERSONAL PROFILE

You are now ready to complete your personal profile. In your journal, list the following:

- Your top three interests.
- Your top three skills and abilities.
- Your top three personal characteristics.

Once you have completed your profile, you can begin listing the kinds of jobs that most closely match your requirements. The more points of your profile a particular job satisfies, the more likely you will be happy working at it.

One of my clients, Paul, uncovered some interesting things about himself while completing this exercise and created what is perhaps one of the more unusual jobs I've heard of. By examining the different areas outlined above—interests, skills, needs and characteristics and combining the answers, Paul was able to design a whole new career path for himself.

Having worked as a manager for a large corporation for most of his adult life, he knew that, after his taking an early retirement, he wanted to do something very non-traditional in his new job. Working through the exercises, Paul identified several components that would make up his ideal work.

He always liked adventure, enjoyed the company of other people and had always been the rugged, outdoor type. People naturally looked to him for leadership and, as a manager, he had developed strong coaching skills. He knew he wanted to work at a job that had little or no routine and would challenge him. However it also had to include a substantial income since he planned to continue his present lifestyle. His personal strengths of being outgoing and energetic were balanced by his deep caring about other people.

One day, while flying cross-country to visit one of his company's field offices, he read an article about a company that marketed "Outward Bound" courses for executives and team-building. "My eyes lit up," he confided to me, "and I knew this was for me. It met almost every criteria I had set for my next career." To make a long story short, he called the company, went in for an interview and was offered a position as one of their team-building trainers. The company felt he was perfect for them, too, especially with his extensive management background.

Test-driving a new career

One way you can "test-drive" a new job is to volunteer to work at the job for a period of time. There are good reasons why college internships are so successful. They allow the people to get a sense of what a particular job is like before asking them to make a long term commitment.

Please keep in mind that your decision is not set in concrete. You are allowed to make career changes and most likely will do so several times in your working life. Earlier generations were taught that a job was "for life," however, in today's workplace people often move through several different careers. As a matter of fact, recent studies reveal that people with too many years in the same company or at the same job are being viewed as unusual. Employers are wondering if there is something wrong with these people since they've been in the same place for a long time. Today's typical employees are in a particular job for an average of five years and that number is decreasing. It's not unusual to find top talent moving from job to job every two years, each time, of course, getting better and better packages.

I once asked two bright, young college graduates, who were working as interns in a county office, about their job expectations and how long they planned to remain in a job once they found what they were looking for. "Three years," replied Mary, without even stopping to ponder the question. "Not me," exclaimed Fran, "I only plan to be in a job for about two years before I move on to something better." Clearly, the idea of a twenty-five year career was not in their reality.

On another occasion, I asked a senior executive friend about his expectations with new hires. His response was even more shocking. He said, with total frankness, that if he could find a capable person who would give him eighteen months of dedicated service, he'd be happy.

MELANIE'S STORY

Melanie is a bright, energetic woman who wanted to add more joy to her work. While she liked her job as a sales representative for a telecommunications company and she earned a sizable income, she felt something was missing. She didn't seem to be fully connected with what she was doing although she did enjoy the interaction with people that the job provided.

After completing her interests and personal profiles, she realized that many of her key interests and abilities were not being utilized. After a day of working in the field in her sales position, she would find herself coming home and surfing the Internet for hours on end—something she really liked. Learning computers had always come easily to her, an unusual trait since most of her generation was computer-phobic.

During the exercises, she remembered a job she had held years ago when she worked as a student teacher while in college. She had enjoyed the teaching assignments and felt good, knowing she was helping people learn. Some of what she learned from these exercises was that, although she enjoyed meeting people and was an effective communicator, she also enjoyed working with computers and could easily learn new technology. Most importantly, she realized that, in order to really be happy in her work and feel fulfilled, she needed to be doing something that was more centered around helping people.

From her company's internal Web site, she learned of an opening as a computer trainer in the HR department. She applied, was awarded the position, transferred within the company and has never looked back. Melanie is happier now since more of her own needs are being met and she's able to use more of her abilities. An added bonus was that she was able to do this without even having to leave the company where she worked for several years. Particularly within larger corporations, this is becoming more of a trend. People are able to stay within the company while finding work that is more acceptable to them. The payoff to the company is that they now have a happier employee who will probably do a better job because she's doing something she truly enjoys. Everyone wins!

SECRET 3: GET TO KNOW
YOURSELF REALLY WELL

*"If you hear a voice saying 'you're not a painter,' then
by all means paint and that voice will be silenced."*

VINCENT VANGOGH

*G*etting to know yourself is one of the best invest-
ments you can make in your future. The better
you know yourself and understand your needs,
wants and desires, the better you will be able to design a life
that you'll truly love. It will be easier for you to make decisions
based on your needs and make choices that will leave you happier and feeling more fulfilled.

One of the reasons so many people are unhappy is that
they really do not know what they want. In my seminars, I
often ask people what they want and am astounded at the
number of blank stares I receive in return. In chapter 5 we will
explore this in more detail but, for now, begin thinking about
what you want and start to make notes in your journal. How
can we expect to have the life of our dreams if we do not invest
the time in identifying what that is?

IDENTIFYING YOUR SKILLS

Identify your skills. Listen to your desires. Write a list of
your needs and wants. Look at the labels you've given your-

self. Embrace your values and special gifts. Celebrate your passions. Liberate yourself from the beliefs you drag around like a ball and chain. While it may sound simple, this step can be quite daunting. As the familiar saying goes, "It's difficult to see the picture when you're inside the frame." You can jump-start this discovery process by partnering with someone who is objective, honest and dedicated to your success, such as a personal coach or a career counselor. Working with a partner dramatically expands your perspective and keeps you anchored as you explore uncharted waters.

IDENTIFYING YOUR PERSONALITY

It is important to consider your personal traits when selecting an occupation so you can avoid trying to be someone you are not.

For example, if you're really shy, a career that involves a lot of public speaking may not be your best choice, unless of course, you plan to train to be a better presenter. To better identify your personality traits, answer the following questions:

What adjectives would you use to describe yourself? What adjectives would your friends, family and employers use to describe you? One of my coaching clients came up with the following list:

Adventurous, caring, confident, creative, enthusiastic, humorous, imaginative, outgoing, punctual, resourceful, strong, sincere, understanding and witty.

Uncovering your values

Some personal insights: I have spent many years reading and attending seminars on "success" and have come away with what works for my own life and what works in helping my clients live a balanced life or a life filled with success. I have seen a few common denominators. These are things that I have incorporated into my day-to-day activities and assist my clients in learning to do the same. They are basic and simple and help us recognize what is most important in our lives.

What are the areas that make-up my idea of "success"? They start with my relationship with Mark, my spouse. This is most important to me. Second is my relationship with my family, then my friends and co-workers.

My career contribution is next on my list as this is something I enjoy and have passion about. Success for me continues by having time for recreation and some form of spiritual practice. I also add learning and finance to the things that are important in my life. And my final components for success are contributions to community, nutrition, and exercise.

These are my life success components. Each day I plan to spend time and focus on the areas that are important to me.

Values are those traits that are near and dear to you. Generally, your values are what you hold in the highest esteem and are the guiding force for your life. Unhappiness and frustration occur when a person's values conflict with his or her lifestyle. This is especially apparent in careers where so many people are doing work that is in opposition to their inner values. For example, if security is one of your major values, you most likely will not want to start a business. On the other hand, if your top values include adventure or challenge, you may be a candidate for entrepreneurship.

The easiest way to identify your (or anyone's) top values is to answer the following question: What is most important to you in your life? If you want to know a person's career values, you can rephrase the question and ask, "What is most important to you in your career?"

Using this simple guide can have a huge impact on your personal relationships and your ability to effectively communicate with others. If, for example, I know that family is one of your highest values and I am trying to recruit you into my company, I will emphasize all the family benefits we offer. On the other hand, if I uncover the fact that your top value is position or money, I will focus on the promotion and financial opportunities available with the company.

Knowing someone's top values makes it possible for you to communicate benefits that are important to them which, in turn, results in more effective communication.

WHAT ABOUT YOU?

Do you know what your own success model is? Consider what areas are most important to you. Is it your children or family or sense of community? Evaluate how much time you want to spend daily with your spiritual practice, career, family, health, etc. Then develop practices that will support your way of living so that you live the life that is your own success.

What are your values? Answering the "What's most important in my life" question for yourself will produce a list of values which may include security, love, money, family, challenge, compassion, contribution, honesty, spirituality and many others. Once you have your list, you can begin to prioritize them in the order that reflects your hierarchy.

For instance, is security more important to you than money? What about family? Is that more important than challenge? Is love more important than security? Is money more important than security?

By understanding the order of your values, you can begin to understand "what makes you tick." You are then in a better position to make choices that are in alignment with who you truly are. You can begin making the kinds of choices that will nourish your true needs and, as a result, you will become happier and more satisfied. When you have your hierarchy of values representing who you are, you're in a better position to evaluate a prospective career or job offer in relation to your own needs and values. By using your list of values, you can design a life that will meet more of your personal needs and, as a result, be happier in whatever you do. Keep in mind that there are some 57,000 different jobs in the US alone!

CHERYL'S LIST

When Cheryl, a high-powered manager, completed this exercise, she learned some very important things about her true desires and core values. Her list had as her number one value, contribution. Her order of importance revealed family, love, prestige, adventure, challenge, money and security to be her other top values. From this list she was able to understand why she always felt better in jobs where she was doing something that had a direct effect on people's lives, even though they paid less or had little security. She also realized that her current job as manager was not meeting her needs since it kept her away from her family for long periods and, although the money and security were there, she did not feel the sense of connection she needed to be truly happy. By uncovering her hierarchy of values, she is better equipped to evaluate her decisions in terms of her own needs. This will result in her making choices that will leave her happier and more fulfilled.

"To find out what one is fitted to do and to secure an opportunity to do it is the key to happiness."

JOHN DEWEY

SKILLS AND APTITUDES

It is human nature to enjoy doing those things we are good at, especially in relation to our work. If you feel you are good at a particular job, you are more likely to enjoy it, therefore, investing the time to identify your skills and aptitudes is time well spent. A thorough skills-analysis is a critical component of your career-planning process.

Skills include the specific aptitudes, talents and personal qualities we bring to a job, as well as the learned procedures the job teaches us and are the building-blocks of your future career.

Your skills and abilities are affected by your personal preferences and you are more likely to be motivated to repeatedly use those skills that are part of enjoyable activities. Your success with particular skills creates your self-motivators, since they are skills you enjoy and are good at.

WORK SKILLS

Your ability to secure and keep a job involves more than just your job skills. In addition to job-related skills, are adaptive skills – the skills that help us cope, shape our attitudes and determine how we manage ourselves and interact with others, and transferable skills – skills that are learned as we experience different situations both within and outside the workplace. These skills can easily be transferred from one situation to another. This is why, for example, a company president is often hired from outside the industry. The fact that she is from another field is secondary since she brings the necessary executive skills to run the company.

ADAPTIVE SKILLS EXERCISE

In your journal, make a list of some of the adjectives that describe your adaptive skills. Your list may include characteristics such as: accepting, adventurous, ambitious, caring, cheerful, committed, confident, dedicated, efficient, energetic, fair-minded, happy, independent, insightful, likeable, objective, orderly, organized, outgoing, patient, precise, productive, receptive, responsive, self-confident, sincere, talented, tolerant, truthful, unique.

TRANSFERABLE SKILLS EXERCISE

Next, in your journal, make a list of some of the adjectives that describe your transferable skills. Your list may include people skills, like assisting, coaching, helping, serving. Information skills like analyzing, calculating, evaluating, organizing and scheduling. Communication skills like advising, interpreting, presenting, talking and writing. Creative skills such as arranging, creating, designing, developing, generating, inventing and producing. Leadership skills like administering, coordinating, directing, facilitating, leading, managing, motivating, planning and supervising. Manual and mechanical skills like constructing, installing, operating, repairing and servicing.

When considering what job-related skills you possess, be sure to consider all of the skills that might relate to a job, even though you may have acquired them from a hobby, volunteer work or previous job. It may be helpful to write out the occupational descriptions from jobs you've had in the past to see what skills you actually used there.

While Susan had worked for many years as a mid-level manager in a bank and had years of experience handling fund-raising and event-planning for her local chapter of the National Association of Women Business Owners. When the time came for her to begin assessing her skills, she drew upon the many talents she had used in her event planning work as well as her managerial experience.

After completing this exercise, she found that she had organizational skills, loved to solve problems and research solutions, and could persuade others to see her point of view. Once she recognized her skills, she knew that in order for her to feel satisfied, her job would need to fulfill her love of problem-solving, persuasion and organizing.

By knowing what interests, skills and talents you possess and what comes naturally to you, you can then honor your own uniqueness. When you "play" all day doing the things you enjoy, work is no longer a task but a natural extension of who you are.

SECRET 4: CREATE A DESTINATION WITH SOUL

"It's a funny thing about life; if you refuse to accept anything but the best, you very often get it."

SOMERSET MAUGHAM

*J*ust as change begins with an ending, change ends with a new beginning. Set your sights on a place where your head is in alignment with your heart. A place built upon the solid foundation of your values, special skills and unique gifts.

SEE IT FIRST

There is a wonderful story about the opening of Disney World in Orlando, Florida. A reporter was interviewing Roy Disney, Walt Disney's brother, and he exclaimed, "It's too bad Walt did not live to see this." Roy quickly replied, "Walt saw it first. That's why you're seeing it now."

Walt Disney had a dream. He was one of the people who had not forgotten how to dream and to dream big. Walt knew that if he could imagine something, if he could dream it, he could make it a reality. The Disney Empire is a true testimony to the effects of a vivid imagination and the benefits of following your dreams.

Imagine you have been given a magic wand and can use it to create whatever future you desire. There are no limits. You can create whatever your heart desires. Use your magic wand now and paint the perfect setting for your future.

Give yourself permission to write down your dreams. Don't skimp on the details. They are often the keys to unlocking joy.

IDEAL LIFE EXERCISE

In your journal, describe your ideal life. What features from your previous jobs do you want to include? How can you best honor your values and share your gifts? How do you want to be spending your time? Who is in your life? How do you feel? What does your typical day look like? What are you doing? What kinds of activities are you engaged in? Who are you interacting with?

Try to describe the general feelings associated with your activities rather than the activities themselves. The more you can gain a sense of the emotions attached to your work, the better you will be able to attract the kind of work you'll love.

You may want to sit quietly, close your eyes and visualize what your ideal work would be like. Try to get a clear picture of yourself in your ideal working environment. The more vivid you can make your images, the clearer you will become about what you actually want to have in your life.

Now that you know who you really are and where you want to go, the next step is getting there.

GOALS MAKE THE DIFFERENCE

It has been said that, "If you don't know where you're going, any road will take you there." Unfortunately, this is true for too many people. Too many of us have never taken the time to learn and apply simple goal-setting principles and as a result, to paraphrase Henry Thoreau, lead lives of quiet desperation.

Interestingly enough, if you survey highly successful people in almost any field, you will find that without exception, they all use goal-setting as part of their success formula. Successful people take the time to set goals and develop plans for their achievement.

Unsuccessful people, on the other hand, just wander through life aimlessly, accepting whatever comes their way. They usually take whatever job is offered them and go through life feeling frustrated and unfulfilled.

If you want to have a more successful and enjoyable life, invest the time to identify and write out your dreams and goals. It's not a difficult process, nor does it require special training or tools to accomplish.

Now that you have a better idea of your skills and desires, it's time to let your creative mind go and really expand your vision. What do you really want? What do you want to have in your life? What kind of person would you like to become? What do you want to do? Where do you want to go?

DREAMS EXERCISE

Sit quietly somewhere you won't be disturbed for a while. Close your eyes and think about everything you want for your life. Really let yourself go and don't be afraid to dream big. Norman Vincent Peale, one of the greatest teachers of the twentieth century, once said, "If you want a big life, you need big dreams!"

As you think about what you want and record your desires in your journal, don't worry about how you will accomplish these things. When the little voice in your head comes in to tell you that something is impossible, silence it just for now. There's always time to deal with "reality." For now, just let your creative mind go and really stretch yourself. If there were no limits, what would you want?

The very word "desire" comes from the Greek meaning "of the Father." It is virtually impossible for you to desire something without also being given the means necessary to attain it.

We all have dreams. Martin Luther King had a dream. John F. Kennedy had a dream. A woman named Anita Roddick, while living in England, had a dream to create a business that would promote the use of all natural beauty products while helping underdeveloped countries and today, there's a Body Shop store in almost every mall in the U.S. You have dreams too and you owe it to yourself to fulfill your dreams.

What do you want? Write in your journal everything you can think of that you want to have, do or become. Invest about twenty minutes doing this. You can always add to it later. As a matter of fact, once you begin letting your imagination go, you will find there are all sorts of things that will come up. You may even remember things from your past that you wanted at one time but have forgotten. Write down everything that comes to you, no matter how unlikely it may seem at the moment. There was a time when I could not have imagined ever leaving my comfortable corporate job and venturing out on my own.

Turning dreams into goals

Once you have your list, you'll want to go back over it and put a check mark next to those items which you feel you can reasonably accomplish in a year or two or those that you feel are truly important. Sailing the high seas may be something you'd like to do "some day," however, having more disposable income may be a higher priority today. Check off what matters to you most in your present life.

Next, on a separate page, write a short sentence that affirms your top four or five goals that you feel you can accomplish in the next six months to a year. Later, you can come back and complete this exercise for any time period from one month to twenty years. It's a good idea to have short, medium and long-term goals as a kind of road map to your future. I'm not suggesting you structure your life in great detail, however, if you have a clear idea of what kind of life you'd like to experience, you greatly increase your potential to bring it about.

A couple of "rules" should be observed whenever you set goals. You'll want to write your goals down. Having a goal that is only in your mind makes it too vague and can easily be forgotten. The simple act of writing down your desires by itself increases their chance of coming to pass. It signals your subconscious mind that you really want this goal.

Next, you want to write your goals in the present tense. If you write them in the future, your subconscious mind will keep them in your future. Affirm them as having already occurred. For example, if one of your goals is to be promoted, you might write, "I am enjoying my new position as vice-president and the challenges it brings."

Be sure to phrase your goal in the positive. Your subconscious does not respond to a negative idea. For example, if you want to lose fifteen pounds, rather than write that you've lost the weight, affirm that, "I am now at my ideal weight of 115 pounds."

Finally, make your goal as specific as you can and, if possible, place a date on it. Having a goal of "more money" is far too vague for the Universe to respond to. A better goal would be, "I am now earning an additional $2,000 a month." You can then add a date when you would like that to occur.

One suggestion is to allow enough time to reasonably accomplish your goal. Saying that you want to have a million dollars by tomorrow is probably a bit too optimistic and will only sabotage your efforts. However, a five-or ten-year goal of becoming a millionaire is more realistic and can be accomplished.

MORE THAN MONEY

If you really want to have the life of your dreams, you'll want to set goals for more than one area of your life. Balance is the key in goal-setting, as it is in life. If all your focus is on work or money at the expense of your family and health, will you be happy? I don't think so. To really have a joyful, fulfilling life you will want to set goals for several areas of your life. The various components that make up your life: spiritual, family, social, mental, emotional, career, finance, health and fitness are all important. It is a good idea to have specific goals in each as a way of creating a really great life.

Concerning all acts of initiative there is one elementary truth, the ignorance of which kills countless ideas and endless plans: That the moment one definitely commits oneself, then providence moves, too.

JOHANN WOLFGANG VON GOETHE

COMMITMENT

It has been said that you can accomplish any goal if you're truly committed. If there is one critical factor that separates people who succeed from people who do not, it's commitment.

IF YOU ARE COMMITTED TO YOUR GOALS, YOU WILL SUCCEED

Regardless of how important a goal is to you, there will come a time when you will become discouraged. Perhaps one of your main goals is going back to school in order to qualify for a better position in your company. Even though it's important to you, there will come a day when you will want to skip a class or even give it up entirely. It is at this time that your level of commitment will come to your rescue. Commitment is what will get you out of bed early on a Saturday morning to make a class, even though you'd rather sleep in. It is commitment that will get you to the gym even after a long hard day at the office and it is commitment to your marriage that will keep your family life intact through the inevitable rough times in any relationship.

GETTING COMMITTED

Now that you realize how important it is to have a strong sense of commitment to accomplish your goals, the big question is how do you do it? It's really very simple. We are driven by one of two things. The desire to gain pleasure or the need to avoid pain. It's the "carrot and the stick" principle that has been used to motivate people for all time. The secret is to take charge of the carrot and stick and use it to motivate yourself.

Go back to your top goals and, on another page in your journal, write a short paragraph describing, in detail, all the benefits you will gain by achieving each particular goal. Really motivate yourself. Focus on the great feelings, the benefits to your family and how much better your life will be when you have accomplished this goal. Do this for each of your major goals.

Next, do the opposite. Write a short paragraph describing what you will lose and what you are already missing out on by not having achieved your goal. Be tough on yourself. Very often we will do more to avoid pain than to gain pleasure so, if you can conjure up enough pain, real or imagined, you will be able to motivate yourself through any situation.

This simple exercise will help get you through the tough times. When you feel like giving up, come back and re-read your reasons for wanting your goals in the first place. As you progress, you can add to your reasons for wanting your ideal life.

To make sure your trip is effortless, do some strategic planning before you start out. When's the best time to begin? Does it make sense to break the journey down into small pieces? What obstacles do you anticipate encountering? What's your plan for navigating around these obstacles? What type of resources do you need? What's a realistic and energizing timeline? How will you gauge your progress? As you head down the road, remember to look around. You don't want to be so focused on your plan that you miss out on wonderful and unexpected opportunities along the way.

DO WHAT YOU LOVE

People who really believe their work is important can often put up with enormous amounts of pressure. Whenever possible, choose work that's personally meaningful to you. Even if that's not possible, you can choose to do your best at the work you've been given.

"A man of knowledge lives by acting, not by thinking about acting"

CARLOS CASTENEDA

GET UP AND GET MOVING

Once you have decided to take responsibility and make changes in your life, it is necessary to take action. You can have all the lofty goals and ambitions you want but until you actually take some action, they remain simply wishes and unfulfilled dreams. The key to all personal power is action.

Make that extra phone call, write that extra letter, or do whatever it is that you have a tendency to avoid doing. Procrastination is surely a death rattle. It will stop us from ever achieving our goals, from ever accomplishing what we want in our lives. It will prevent us from ever having that which we want and deserve for ourselves and our loved ones. In order to live fully, you must end procrastination — now. Don't be like the guy who was going to start a club for procrastinators but decided to wait.

How many times have you had an idea at work and hesitated, only to watch someone else make the suggestion and receive the credit for it? Let me ask you a question. What was the difference between your idea and the person who actually implemented it? I'm sure you have already guessed it. They took action. It's that simple. Action. The way to realize the power and potential you have is to take action.

Once you have decided on your goals, and written them down, write down the action steps you will need to take to reach your target.

Be sure to include one or two things you can do right now, today, to get yourself moving toward your new goal. Doing something immediately brings into being the law of physics that says an object in motion tends to stay in motion until acted upon by an outside force. By taking the first step, however small, you are putting yourself and your talents in motion and, before you realize it, you will have reached your destination.

SECRET 5: ENJOY THE JOURNEY

*T*here is no denying fear. It's perfectly natural for you to have fears associated with your life, especially your career. It is natural. Someone who tells you they have no fears is either lying to you or living in denial. However, your fears do not need to prevent you from making your life everything you want it to be.

OVERCOMING YOUR FEARS

It has been said that fear is just "False Evidence Appearing Real." For the most part, this is true. Most of what we fear does not exist. Too many people are holding themselves back from the life they truly want because they have fears about the outcome of their actions. While the fears are real, the basis for the fear is generally an illusion.

You avoid making a telephone call for a new job because you fear the possibility of rejection on the other end of the line. You don't ask that special person out on a date for fear of rejection. You fear taking on a new project because you are afraid you will not perform up to par.

Looking at each of these situations realistically, we can see that the fear is baseless. In the example of the telephone call, the chances of being accepted are at least as good as the chance of rejection. If you're calling about the right job, the chance of a warm reception is even greater. Successful actors, models and salespeople have learned that rejection is just part of the process and take it in stride.

In the case of the dinner date, it's even simpler. If you don't ask the person out, you're not having dinner with them anyway. You can't lose, other than a slight bruise to your ego. Even then, if your self-image is intact, you can reframe the experience and see it as the other person's loss.

Your reluctance to take on a new project for fear of failure is probably just not true. If you are being considered for a project in the first place, your boss has the belief in your ability to accomplish the task. It is your own lack of confidence that's holding you back.

It has been said that if you do that which you fear, the death of fear is certain. Of course, I'm not suggesting you take unnecessary or dangerous risks. That's not facing fear. That's foolishness. What I am suggesting, however, is that, presuming you are properly prepared or trained for a situation, you put your fears aside and just go for it.

You cannot ignore or deny the fact that you have fears about a particular situation but you do not have to be immobilized by it. Just acknowledge the fear and move past it. It's like Susan Jeffers says in her book, *Feel the Fear and Do It Anyway*.

OPENING DOORS TO YOUR FUTURE

Throughout our lives, we continue to make many new

discoveries about ourselves and the world. We may find that we have changed and want different things or our view of the world may have changed or even the world itself has changed. When faced with a changing work environment, it's normal to experience mixed emotions. If you are laid off or your hours, salary and benefits are cut, or if your colleagues are suffering these things, your first reaction may be that the future of your job is in question. What if you began to accept that while the change may be closing one door, a new door is opening? What if you viewed the new door as one of opportunity? A door that leads to a life in which you have complete control over your career and can design a career that is in harmony with who you are and what you want your life to be like. Now, that's an exciting prospect!

Once we begin to learn what we really want for ourselves in our careers, then we can explore what the world has to offer. Because so much of our life is spent at work, thinking about work or preparing for work, career decisions are one of the most important decisions for us to make. Use times of change to begin to discover more about yourself and the world around you. This process of self-discovery can be joyful and relieve the stress you are feeling about not being in control of your destiny.

THE JOURNEY BEGINS

The first step is to discover who you are and what you really want to do. Begin thinking about the things you do that bring you delight. What are your favorite hobbies? What would you like to do every day even if no one paid you for it? Answer the following: If you knew you could not fail and money did not matter, what great things would you attempt to do?

Your true passion lies in this answer. It may have been buried down deep by the things you tell yourself, such as, "I should be a lawyer forever. That's what I went to school for."

I give you permission to put these types of myth aside and begin to enjoy finding what you really want to do. So stop telling yourself that your career choice is a life-time commitment – it certainly isn't unless you choose it to be. It is also unfair to believe that the career you selected when you were 17 or 20 is the one that fits you and brings you personal fulfillment when you are 30, 40 or 50. What about the message you give yourself when you tell yourself that you should have selected the perfect career that was guaranteed into the future? I don't have a crystal ball and neither do you. You made the best choice at the time, with the information you had. Now you have the opportunity to make another choice if you want to.

The final myth I want you to push aside is the one that says a career is a linear and upward process. Is certainly doesn't have to be. What if you were the president of a company and then found you didn't like it? Do you think it is wrong for someone to find it doesn't suit them and take a job further down the ladder? Career satisfaction is personal satisfaction. It is not about moving up the ladder to please others. Begin making yourself happy.

The reality of careers is that opportunity and change are constant. You can't control them. All you can do is make a long-term commitment to life-long learning and understand that change is essential. You can also begin to see that your value and who you are as a person are separate from your career. Paid employment of any type at any level is only one small aspect of your personal fulfillment. It is not your life. Just as there are no guarantees in life, there are also no assurances in careers. We are living in a time of tremendous restructuring in the workplace and we can choose to accept this and see our careers as cyclical, sometimes lateral and always evolving but never predictable.

"If you are what you do, then when you don't, you aren't."

WAYNE DYER

Here are some concepts that will help you keep your career development process in perspective. Realize that change is constant. As humans we have a wonderful ability to adapt and to keep gaining knowledge. It is up to us to search for and to create our own opportunities. We need to move away from the belief in stable jobs and companies and realize we can continue to evolve. It is critical that we listen to our own inner voices, hear our own passions and follow our own hearts. Our dreams and our wishes are what brings guidance to our careers. Stating our needs, values, interests and beliefs and fully realizing them and acknowledging them will allow us to create the vision for where we want to go. It is up to us where we go. We are no longer just pulled along.

EMBRACE THE MAGIC

Embrace the magic of this journey. Every time you listen to your heart, put aside a myth, or make a choice, you are becoming empowered. Life is a wonderful journey that is meant to be enjoyed. You now have the opportunity to really get to know the inner you—the part of you that had a vision but wasn't willing to share it because of the myths that you once believed. This is the time to remember how to dream and how to use your creativity to fulfill your vision.

As you embark upon this journey, open your eyes and your heart to your personal assets and ask yourself how they might transfer to a career that you love. The goal of the journey is find the work you love and love the work you do so that doing it is something you would choose even without a paycheck. Instead of feeling helpless and finding it difficult to accept what your present life has become, take control and then assure yourself that change is a way of learning. Take responsibility for your own learning. The message is that we need to be aware and we need to be ready for change. It is up to you to take action and to move yourself forward.

During this journey, reach out and ask for help. Asking for help is not a sign of weakness but a sign of inner strength. Seek new resources, make new contacts and use them. You have many allies in your life. If you need help with the tools and strategies for making the career journey, seek the help of a career coach to help you take the initiative.

WORK YOURSELF HAPPY

Finding a career that matches your own personal interests and abilities is a wonderful process. When you know yourself and understand your own interests, values, needs and abilities, then work becomes a way to express yourself and present yourself to the world. It becomes a way to share your interests and your talents. Since you now realize that your interests and skills can change over time, you can begin to understand that when they do, you can move on to another occupation that will again fulfill you. If work is not about a job but about doing something that makes you happy, then it is easy to understand that having different careers over the course of a lifetime is perfectly acceptable.

When you first chose your profession, had you considered your interests, abilities, and values? Did you explore the alternatives thoroughly? Many times people come to a career coach without knowing how or why they ended up in a given career or unaware of what to do when their field or they change. If your goal is to be happy doing what you enjoy and your work is a way of expressing yourself, then you will expect work to be a wonderful, exciting place where you can be happy.

Begin to live your life, not the one that has been expected of you. Do work that matches your values and work that brings you energy and fulfillment. People who work themselves happy are people who are drawn to their work naturally. It brings them delight and they have enthusiasm for what they do. Don't just let your fantasies slip away. Open the door, discover the journey, embrace the magic and work yourself happy.

BALANCE

Below are two examples of people who learned, through personal coaching, how to put more balance in their lives. You can do the same, with or without a coach. While working with a personal coach is great, if you cannot do this right now, you can learn to be your own coach and create the same type of balance you need.

Alice is a very intelligent CEO of a healthcare corporation who was feeling burned-out in her career. She had just gone through a divorce and decided that she no longer wanted a career that did not allow her time for family. She worked so many hours and under such pressure that she missed many meals and often ate junk food for dinner. She was missing the things she loved like exercise and hobbies. She nearly cried when I told her I wanted her to take vacations and to have some form of fun every day — something she could look forward to more than work every single day.

We worked on planning her days to include very strong boundaries around her work time. I had her develop and stick to a rigid schedule where she left the office by 6:00. We scheduled a routine for her taking lunch and 2 breaks to walk outdoors every day. She was consistent in doing this although she felt very selfish at first. In addition, we looked at her calendar, which was full of meetings. I helped her decide which were necessary and which could be shortened or eliminated. We then worked on her giving up tasks and projects and delegating them to others as well as dropping many projects and opportunities that came her way. She began declining social obligations that she did not enjoy and only accepted those she felt passionate about. She began to listen to her own inner voice and let go of the need to always be perfect.

In the office she planned quiet time to think, to slow down and to plan. She closed the door, let voice mail take her calls and asked not to be interrupted during these times. This was a huge shift for her.

Although when she came to me she was sure she wanted to change jobs she learned she could stay at the job she had because we re-designed the job so that it wasn't killing her. She now goes to the gym every day, enjoys her job, gets home earlier, enjoys lunches with co-workers or quiet walks. She talks, lives and works more slowly. She works 45 hours (down from 65 per week) and has balance in her life. The burnout is gone and she is very satisfied with her career.

Michael, an IT professional, is in a mid-level position in a company that is undergoing major change. Much of this revolves around the fact the company is owned by a foreign conglomerate and there is a cultural struggle. He has had a poor review and bad feedback and feeling unwelcome and unwanted in the company and knows he wants to leave. When he came to me he said he had decided to throw in the towel and resign. I requested that he first get away from the situation and take time off. I encouraged him to redo his work schedule to include time every day for embracing his hobbies—gardening and music—and spending time with his spouse. Also, we analyzed what he needs from the company to feel more respected. I helped him schedule a conversation with his boss, co-workers and subordinates, about his needs. He was direct and unemotional with them after having been away for some time.

He managed to remain at work and felt less stress being there and, although he still wants another job, he doesn't feel such pressure to get out, especially without having another job. He is pursuing his hobbies and interests while he is updating his resumé. He is not feeling the same pressure to find a new job immediately. He has gained a new balance in his life and has been able put work in its proper perspective. It is no longer how he measures his self-worth. He has learned that he wants a career that allows him more time for his hobbies and more balance in his life—a career with a company that will give him the respect he deserves.

Your story

What about you? How balanced is your life? Do you spend all your time and energy working? Do you allow enough time for your personal needs and your family? What about vacations? When was the last time you took a "real" vacation?

There's an email circulating that, among other things, suggests that you "know when you're working too much when you get up in the middle of the night to go to the bathroom and check your email before returning to bed." Unfortunately, this is becoming all too true.

Extraordinary self-care

"I take pretty good care of myself." How many times have you said that? You think to yourself, "I'm taking pretty good care of myself. After all, I eat well and exercise a bit. Why do I need to do more?"

What I'm suggesting here is that you take this idea to a whole new level. It's called *Extraordinary self-care* and it involves learning how to take really good care of yourself. You're worth it. I'm talking about things beyond the basics of self-care. I'm talking about really nurturing yourself and making a habit of doing things that are really good for you. Things that make you feel great.

This may begin sounding a little narcissistic but it's

important to learn to take great care of yourself as part of your overall plan to have a more joyful and happy life.

Stephanie, the owner of a computer software training business, no longer enjoys her own business or her profession. She hated the changes brought about by corporate downsizing and the struggle it has become to collect accounts receivable. She doesn't want to own a business anymore and came to me for help in selling her company.

Her vision was to close the doors and run away quickly to a quieter world.

I sensed that she was physically and mentally tired so we began coaching with a program anchored in extraordinary self-care. This included daily exercise, eating healthy food, and taking a vacation right in the middle of this mess. I also requested that she say no to new projects because she was too drained to give of herself at the time.

Her partner wanted her to sell while her gut was telling her to just walk away, be "poor" and be happy. She struggled with this after years of building the business. After all, it was her baby and her blood, sweat and tears. I encouraged her to put together a support team consisting of myself, her life partner, a couple of close friends and her sister. I sug- gested she ask them to support her with her decision. What happened is that some of the team members and other friends and professionals tried to tell her what she should do. They suggested she stick it out and keep her business or at least wait until she could get "the best offer." She told me that some even got angry, and tried to make her feel guilty. I helped her to learn to listen to her own voice. By answering questions and writing in her journal, she allowed her real feelings to come out. She knew that she could be a trainer for some other company or even freelance. She just wanted to shut down and end this career that was eating up her life. She heard, in her heart, that she didn't want to wait for a sale so she decided to go against the wishes of some of her support team. She walked away and never looked back. She shut the doors, took a wonderful vacation and is now working for someone else, feeling more energy and zest. She told me she felt close to a breakdown and if she hadn't said no to what everyone else wanted and found a way to stand up for herself, she would have lost her life to her business.

EXTRAORDINARY SELF-CARE EXERCISE

How many of the following do you perform at least monthly?
Have a facial
Get a massage
Walk in nature
See a movie

Take a day off
Reconnect with someone special
Reconnect with you
Wear something you feel great in
Take a field trip to somewhere you always wanted to visit
Get in touch with culture: visit a museum, gallery
Review your goals
Give some time to someone who needs help

How many of the following do you perform at least weekly?

Shine your shoes
Have a manicure (yes, men too)
Write your goals
Take a sauna or sit in a hot tub
Write a letter
Forgive someone
Get sweaty
Have a nice meal prepared by someone else
Dance
Play a sport
Enjoy your hobby
Enjoy fun exercise
Enjoy sunlight
Walk in the park
Read a book
Play with toys
Play with children
Play with a pet
Be with friends
Go for 24 hours with no voice mail
Enjoy flowers
Indulge in a taste treat
Take a long, relaxing bath

How many of the following do you perform daily?

Flossing
Scalp massage
Eating fresh fruit and vegetables
Sit in silence
Let off steam
Wear comfortable clothes and shoes
Move your body
Be silly
Eat 3 meals
Eat healthy foods you love
Call a friend
Be with nature
Listen to music
Be grateful
Drink water—plenty of water
Get 6-8 hours sleep
Get hugged and give hugs
Watch less television
Sing out loud
Laugh out loud
Say no to someone or something
Do something very kind for someone else
Read your goals

Learning to take extraordinarily good care of yourself is a big step toward feeling better about your life. You will learn to cherish and respect your needs and wants. Too many people put everyone else first. Children, spouses, friends, jobs, social commitments, volunteer projects and all the rest of life's complexities tend to take us away from recognizing our own true needs. Often we, by virtue of our active lives, come last in the list of who gets what. This is not always healthy.

I'm not suggesting you neglect your family and career commitments, but that you keep them in balance. I'm suggesting you learn to set aside time for your needs. Learn to recognize when you need nurturing and special time for yourself.

There is an old song lyric that sums it up, "You can't love anyone until you love yourself."

LIFE 101 — SUGGESTIONS FOR A HAPPIER LIFE

"Lighten up" is becoming a popular phrase these days and for good reason. We're all becoming too serious. When was the last time you had a really good laugh? When was the last time you laughed at yourself?

Most of us have a tendency to take ourselves much too seriously. We fret over everything we do as if we're supposed to be perfect in whatever we attempt. So many of us put ourselves down at the slightest imperfection. We say things like, "I'm so stupid. How did I ever get so dense," or, "I'm a dummy, I'll never learn that."

People who live very long lives, such as those over 100 years old, all seem to share a healthy sense of humor. A sense of humor about oneself and the world in general is one of the keys to aging successfully and has been documented in numerous studies.

Laughter is being used to effectively help treat serious illnesses and is even becoming part of the workplace as we realize the importance of taking ourselves more lightly.

The fact that one of the most sought after seminar topics on the speaking circuit is "Humor in the Workplace" attests to our need to learn to put more humor in our lives.

How about you? Can you look at a situation and see the

humor in it? I'm not trying to diminish those issues that are genuinely serious and need to be treated as such; however, you can make your life happier simply by trying to see the humor in many of life's challenging situations.

Humor is healthy. Learning to laugh at your human frailties and less-than-perfect attempts at everyday life is a healthy practice that's well worth developing.

The next time you make some small mistake, instead of berating yourself and calling yourself stupid, try making light of it. Say something like, "Isn't that funny how I have trouble with computers. I'm sure I can learn to do it with a little practice." Not being a technology wizard isn't usually a life-threatening issue.

Make an effort to see the humor in everyday occurrences and you will begin feeling better about yourself and your work. Lighten up and laugh a little. One of the reasons angels can fly is that they take themselves lightly.

KAIZEN

Shortly after the end of World War II, General Douglas McArthur requested that a man named W. Edwards Demming come to Japan to help rebuild that war-torn country. Demming had developed a system called Total Quality Management or TQM.

When the Japanese business leaders met with Dr.

Demming and asked him what he thought they could do to restore their economy, his answer was that they should strive to "make small, incremental improvements daily in every area of their lives and their business." The Japanese word for this is *Kaizen* and it is responsible for the fact that, today, Japan is a world power and economic leader. In Japan there is an award given to the business who has demonstrated the greatest improvement in a given year. It's the "Demming Award."

It's interesting to note that it was not until many years later that Dr. Demming's work was recognized in the United States. His TQM principles are now used by many successful US corporations, including the Ford Motor Company and the Department of the Navy.

You can practice kaizen in your daily life, too. It's a simple concept that, over time, will produce awesome results. I challenge you to practice this idea for 30 days and see for yourself the amazing results.

KAIZEN EXERCISE

For the next 30 days, strive to make small incremental improvements in every area of your life. Each day, begin by asking yourself the following:

How can I improve my relationship with my spouse and family?

How might I improve my health?

What can I do today to improve my value to my company?

How can I improve my sense of enjoyment and pleasure?

What else can I improve today?

I'm not asking you to make major changes or to add stress to your life. I'm simply suggesting that you look at your life and your daily activities and see what small actions you can take — today — that will make your life happier and more joyful. Keep in mind that "progress, not perfection" is what life's all about.

SARAH'S STORY

Sarah is a successful real estate/mortgage industry professional who came to me when she was in the process of finding a new position. While she loved her job and made a very high six-figure income, her company was merging. As we were working on her game plan to stay in the same field, her company went bankrupt. She was shocked and scared and wanted to take the first job that came along.

I encouraged her to recognize that she had expectations of her employers and when she interviewed to put her interests first rather than selling them on her. I told her to hire her own employer and to be choosy. We came up with strategies for her to know what she wanted from an employer and she went on interviews with this intent.

One of her new-found items is she doesn't want to work past

7:00 pm in the evening or on weekends. She communicated this in her interviews. She also wanted to go to her child's class trips and plays and wanted the flexibility to do so.

She was scared this would prevent her from finding a job. Instead, much to her surprise, she received four offers and had to decide which she wanted.

She now spends weekends with her child and evenings at the gym, movies or with friends. Her life is filled with good music, friends, an environment she loves to live in. She let go of working on weekends and takes a break from voice mail and email, to allow herself an escape from work, for one 24-hour period each weekend.

She has had the most successful year of her working life in terms of salary and career satisfaction while living her life on her own terms, earning the highest pay for less time worked.

Tom's story

Tom is the manager of local branch of a national retail chain who came to me having just been put on probation. He feared losing his job and was miserable. He was overworked, stressed, and he had a poor attitude because of his co-workers and his manager. I requested that before he look for another job, he restructure his present job with strong boundaries so that his employees are solving problems, doing their own work and being accountable. I helped him to train them in the skills they lacked and taught him to delegate so that he had less work and wasn't putting in all those crazy hours.

Even after following my suggestions, he still decided he wanted out of this job because he wasn't enjoying being in management or working for the company. He began a career search around the hobbies he loved and decided the money was not as important as his health and well-being.

He found that he could get a job at a lower salary in a field he liked and he decided to accept this offer. The company was one he felt good about working for and he would have no management responsibility. The starting salary is lower but his wife decided to take on a bit more work to compensate. Now the stress is gone and I hear him laughing more, looking better and sounding lighter!

JESSICA'S STORY

This Director of Nursing says she wanted to get away from being indoors all day and working late hours. She thinks she wants to be a consultant. She is struggling with this because she feels she can't give up her job security. I encouraged her to speak with her current employer about going from employee to consultant. She did this and the employer agreed. Now she works less hours for more money and sets her schedule around walking every morning and evening. She is always home by 4:00 pm and is expanding her personal relationships outside work because she finally has time to do this.

She knew just what she wanted to do but couldn't see how to make it happen. She thought her idea was a dream and that her employer would fire her but when she finally got the courage to express her desire, he honored it and she is now working the way she envisioned.

STRESS

If there's one area you must learn to handle if you are to have a happier life at work or otherwise, it's stress. Extreme levels of negative stress can kill you. I say *negative* stress because a certain amount of stress is necessary. The only people who have no stress in their lives are six feet under the earth.

Stress is what gets us going. A certain amount of pressure is healthy and can bring out the best in people. The problem is that our present-day society has taken stress to dangerous levels. Our fast-paced lives, job pressures, the environment, our usually less than ideal diet and lifestyles, all lead to an excess of stressors in most of us.

If you want to learn to live and work yourself happy, you must find ways to cope with the stress in your life. Meditation, hobbies, exercise, yoga, nature walks, friends, family and even our pets can help us manage our daily stress. In the next few pages are some thoughts and ideas to help you get started. If you want to learn more, a visit to your local bookstore will provide you with many books dealing with stress in great detail. Also, your local adult eduction center most likely has a class or two on managing stress. Select activities that work for you. We are all different and what works for me may not be ideal for you.

STEPS TO REDUCE STRESS

- Get up 15 minutes earlier every morning so you can relax before leaving the house.
- Exercise daily to unwind.
- Make a habit of taking long, deep breaths regularly.
- Eliminate the words "ought" and "should" from your vocabulary and make your goals things you really want to do.
- Skip the daily news - it's full of negative events.
- Drive slowly and listen to music while you drive.
- Meditate or sit quietly for a few minutes every day.
- Schedule plenty of time between appointments so you don't feel rushed.

BE STILL AND KNOW

The regular practice of meditation has been shown to be significant in decreasing stress. This is not something that needs to be complicated. Just sit quietly and watch your thoughts. Try not to get caught up in your thinking but instead just become the silent observer. If you want, you can observe your breathing as it goes in and out. Just sit quietly and let go of your thoughts. With regular practice, you will soon sense the "chatter" in your mind subsiding and begin to feel calmer. This feeling will stay with you as you go on with your daily activities.

Some people prefer to take a class to learn a specific technique. If this appeals to you, go for it. Also, you may want to play peaceful music during your periods of quiet reflection. Experiment with different techniques until you find what works for you. An investment of twenty minutes a day in quiet time will pay you back in renewed energy and sense of wellness.

TIME MANAGEMENT

We all have the very same twenty four hours in a day, yet some people are able to accomplish an enormous number of tasks while others never seem to have enough time.

Why do some people seem to have more time than others? The answer is very simple. They manage their time better. Now, I like being spontaneous as much as the next person, however, it is important to employ some system of time-management if you want to feel more in control of your life and get more done.

Organizing your time is a sure way to feel as though you have more of it. While there are numerous time-management books, tapes and seminars, one of the simplest productivity techniques I ever learned is the following:

List the five most important things you have to do and do nothing else until you complete them. I realize that this sounds overly simple in our exceedingly complicated world, but before you dismiss it, try it out for two weeks. This simple technique, which has been used by high-level executives, entrepreneurs, and others, for more than fifty years, works. One of the keys is that by listing five items instead of ten or twenty, you are really focusing your energy on what is truly important. If you eliminate distractions and do only the five items on your list, you will be directing your energy in the most productive direction. Rather than waste your valuable time doing busy work, you will be doing what really matters to your success. Of course, if you complete your list early, write another one, or do other less important tasks.

HEALTH

There is a revolution taking place in the United States

with regard to healthcare. No longer are people willing to sit idly by and follow "doctor's orders." I am not suggesting you do not listen to your doctor, however, it is time you took an active role in your own health.

Learn to ask questions. Do not be afraid to ask for a second opinion. There are still medical practitioners who will not answer their patients questions and, worse yet, patients who still go to these people. Where your health is concerned, you have a right to know. Make sure your medical practitioner takes the time to explain the problem and make sure you are satisfied with the answers.

Every year in the United States billions of dollars are being spent on alternative medicine. The majority of this was out-of-pocket expenses. Clearly, people are taking their medical care into their own hands.

YOUR HEALTH TEAM

Something that is becoming commonplace in our society is the idea of a "health team." Rather than place the responsibility for your health on your doctor, you can assemble your own "team" of practitioners to help you remain in optimum health. Your team may include different specialists such as an internist, a chiropractor, nutritionist, a personal trainer, coach, and other specialists who can help you stay healthy and fit.

"By your thoughts you are daily, even hourly, building your life;
you are carving your destiny."

RUTH BARRICK GOLDEN

WHAT ARE YOU TELLING YOURSELF?

What do you say to yourself on a regular basis? Do you praise yourself for a job well-done and accept your errors as just being human or do you have a habit of putting yourself down for every little thing?

It saddens me when I see so many people telling themselves they're "dumb" or "stupid" or in some other way, putting themselves down. This is one of the most destructive things you can do and it will undermine your success.

We are only human. We will make mistakes and, yes, some of us will have a hard time adapting to new technology or learning to play golf or whatever it is we personally find difficult. This does not make us less intelligent than the rest of the people. We all make mistakes.

Learn to allow yourself errors. Try not to be so hard on yourself and those around you. Your self-talk, that mental chatter that goes on all day long, has a lot to do with your level of achievement. Your subconscious mind does not know the difference between real and imaginary. It will believe and act upon whatever commands you give it.

TRANSFORMATIONAL VOCABULARY

This is simply a fancy word for a concept that was studied several years ago and reported in Time magazine. It means transforming the words you use to describe your experience of any given situation or emotion.

If you want to feel better, use words that amplify your good feelings. For example, if someone asks how you are, instead of saying *fine* or *ok*, try saying *great* or *terrific*. This simple change in your choice of wording will change the way you feel.

In contrast, if you want to feel less poorly about an undesirable occurrence, reduce the impact of the words you use. Rather than saying something like, "I hate my job," change the wording to minimize their impact. You might say, "I'm not really fond of my job." While it expresses the same dislike for the job, the emotional impact is much less, resulting in your feeling better about the situation.

By reducing the impact of the words we use to describe unpleasant situations and enhancing the intensity of those we use to describe pleasant feelings or situations, you will begin to feel better and happier about your life.

LIFE AS AN ENTREPRENEUR

ost entrepreneurs I coach tell me that they want to simplify their life. They are consumed with details, many of which don't seem that critical, yet still have to get done. They also say that they feel their life is out of balance. They live separate business and personal lives and often feel guilt over not being with their families and friends more frequently.

Here are some tips that entrepreneurs I coach have shared as part of their success in building more success at less cost:

1. Get rid of anything and anyone you are tolerating.

2. Get rid of clients that you don't enjoy working with.

3. Plan one hour a day of quality free time just for you.

4. Surround yourself with people who are talented and highly-motivated.

5. Work to free yourself of interruptions.

6. Delegate non-moneymaking activities.

7. Get a coach.

As an entrepreneur, it is critical to simplify your life and focus on your uniqueness and what it is you want to create in your lifetime. Is it relationships, an organization, money, recognition, a new method? Don't forget your life's purpose and mission, along with your business goals. Next, begin focusing on slowing your pace and planning your days, weeks, months and your activities and achievements. Take control of the chaos, slow the activity and improve the results. Organize your work around teams. Those who are supported by others have an extraordinary advantage in all situations in life. Focus only on business tasks that others cannot do for you.

Got a goal? Great. Now expand it, push it, grow it huge! Visualize it and articulate it to others and develop a framework to get results. Instead of focusing on marketing and sales as a singular item, focus on the creation of extraordinary value. Learn to bring to others ever-increasing value and you will have a powerful business. Transform your products into services, services to products, and products and services into a unique experience. This will differentiate you in the marketplace and allow you to be creative.

SELF EMPLOYMENT OPTIONS—WHAT ARE YOUR NEEDS?

Identify Your Needs: When looking at resources to see if you are suited to self-employment or entrepreneurship, consider these questions:

- What are your personal goals?

- What kind of lifestyle would you prefer to lead?

- Can you make decisions and carry them out quickly and effectively?

- Do you have the capacity for hard work and long hours?

- Are you good at setting and meeting goals?

- Do you have the necessary level of training?

- Do you know enough about what is involved in setting up and running a business?

- Are you self-confident?

- Do you mind taking risks?

- Are you good at problem-solving?

- Can you cope with failure?

- Are you a self-starter?

BARBARA'S STORY

Barbara was a former executive secretary with a national company and had held her position for almost 20 years. The company went through a major reorganization and she was downsized. She started coaching with me before her severance ran out and was in the process of starting her own business as an executive assistant. She did not want to work in an office but wanted to become a freelancer so she could work for people anywhere in the world, by computer, phone and fax, as their virtual assistant.

She was a bit panicked because her severance was running out, so I encouraged her to take the pressure off and begin work at a part-time job where she could meet other people for networking purposes, pull in income to take the pressure off, and do something mindless so she could focus on building her business.

Her dream was to have her own business and she had a lot of fear about making it, being successful, being too old to do this and not bringing in the income she wanted to and that she and her husband were used to. As I worked with her to develop a budget and to set aside income each month for her business and also to decrease her household expenses, she was able to feel better about making the full change to her own business. Coaching sessions focused on her passion about her business, overcoming her fear of rejection and of selling, developing strategies to network and meet new people who could use her services and developing a client base. Once she had a small client base I coached her to take the leap and give up the "boring" day job to really fully develop her own business. She was frightened and needed a "loving" push ... she took the plunge in January and is happy in her business; it is growing and she is learning to be less stressed about bringing in fewer dollars and enjoying her life more. She now has hobbies, fits in exercise and spends more time with her family.

FRED AND JEAN'S STORY

Fred and Jean are involved in network marketing and have been for many years. They are very passionate about their business and products and sell a great deal of them but needed to build an organization. That part of the business was going nowhere. They had been unable to recruit very many people and the few they had were not working out. This was causing them to feel burned-out and they were becoming disillusioned with the entire business.

I helped them complete a values and needs assessment which showed them they did have passion about the business and wanted to make it work. They recognized that they were poor at follow-up, unmotivated and didn't have the organizational *tools or time-management skills they needed. I helped them develop the tools to become better organized and assisted them in creating schedules which would enable them to get in front of a set number of people in a given week.They learned to find new ways to tell people about their business, ways which felt natural and didn't seem like a hard-selling sales pitch.*

They were able to recruit a large down-line in a short period of time and they realized that this was, in fact, the business they really wanted and they did want to work at it together. With their new-found passion, it was easier for them to work on their business in ways that felt right for their personalities and fulfilled their individual needs.

TURNING A HOBBY INTO A BUSINESS

Julie had always loved making silver and semi-precious stone jewelry. She made it for friends and gave it as gifts for special occasions. As the result of an accident, she was not able to work for a long period of time. During this recovery period and to avoid becoming depressed, she went to her hobby and started making more jewelry. Her friends suggested she take it to some of the local stores since it was so unique. Interestingly enough, some of the major boutiques in Los Angeles began to carry her work and many of the big-name movie stars began wearing it. Today, Julie has a thriving business and is pursuing her life-long dream of being a jewelry designer. There are countless other similar stories of people following their passion. Do you have a hobby that you could turn into a business? Often it is those things we do for the pure joy of it that become our greatest accomplishments.

Part-time Entrepreneurship

Another alternative and one that is less risky is to begin your business on a part-time basis. Many people are attracted to network marketing and direct sales because these kinds of businesses are designed for people who want to "ease into" their business. They give you the opportunity to try your hand at entrepreneurship without risking your present job security.

Going for it all

Maybe you're ready to take the plunge and "go for it all." If this is the decision you have made there are a few suggestions that can make your transition easier. For one thing, you'll want to have set aside several months worth of living expenses to allow your new venture to get off the ground. If possible, have six months to a year's worth of living expenses in your account before you jump ship. Next, you'll want to have lined up one or two potential customers. Sometimes it can even be your former employer. There are numerous companies who first began as an outsource to their former employer. As a matter of fact, if you see the writing on the wall that your department is being shut down, you may consider approaching your boss with the idea of helping you set up an outsource company to become the vendor to your company. After all, who is better equipped to handle the work? You know the company. You're familiar with all the nuances of the work and you have the industry knowledge. You are in a perfect position to become the new vendor.

There are numerous books available to help you get started in your new business. All you have to do is peruse the shelves of your local bookstore. Also, there are government agencies who will offer you assistance and in many cases free advice from people who are experts in whatever field you are entering. The agency SCORE, Service Core of Retired Executives, offers free help to new businesses. Their members are all former executives who volunteer their time to help new business owners get started. You will find them in your local telephone directory. Another place to look for help is the Small Business Administration (SBA). Their Web site is http://www.sba.gov. You will usually find state and local information on the Internet. You can go to http://www.state.*(your two letter state code)*.us. For example, in Pennsylvania it is: *http://www.state.pa.us*

BECOMING A MORE
VALUED EMPLOYEE

hat if you don't want to leave your present job or start your own business? What if you're reasonably happy right where you are but want to increase your value to your company?

Whenever a company decides to downsize, they usually look around to see who they can easily do without. Some companies use downsizing as a way to get rid of people they don't want or to replace highly-paid workers with seniority with younger people who earn less. Whichever the case, they rarely allow their most valued employees to leave.

One of the keys to always being in demand is to continue to add more value to your position. The better qualified you are, the more in demand you will be so that no matter what happens, you'll land on your feet.

WE'RE ALL SELF-EMPLOYED

In today's workplace, we are all essentially self-employed. You may work for a company but your value to that company and your value in the marketplace are based on your skills and knowledge. While it is true that your skills have been of value to the company up until now, that does not necessarily mean they will be tomorrow and beyond. Unless you take it upon yourself to be responsible for your own personal development, you run the risk of becoming obsolete one day.

If you want to have security in your career, consider yourself an independent human resource who is employed by your company and receives payment for services rendered. By doing this and taking responsibility for your professional growth, you will be sure to do whatever is necessary to maintain your skills value to your current or any future employer.

People who follow this approach take charge of their own careers, upgrading their skills and learning new technology as it appears. They are the people who attend seminars, whether or not the company pays the fee. They utilize the latest tools available to assist them in their work and they are constantly engaged in a program of personal or professional development.

Not coincidentally, these are the same people who are always the last to be let go in a downsizing and sought out by the top companies. Become one of these people and you'll never have to worry about your future security.

CONTINUE TO LEARN FOR LIFE

"I am still learning"

MICHELANGELO

Too many people feel that once they finish their formal education, they can stop learning. Nothing could be further from the truth. As the quote above reminds us, we are always learning. Whatever your age or situation, if you make learning a part of your life, you will be happier, more productive and have a continuous supply of interesting experiences.

CONTINUING EDUCATION AND TRAINING

Education and training are the formal processes by which you acquire knowledge and skills that can help you get and keep a job. Nearly all jobs require you to have some training and, increasingly, a single course or program of training will not be enough for your entire working life.

Decide on your objective. What are your needs? Identify your skills, abilities, career goals, financial situation, etc. Set educational goals for the short-term and long-term.

Identify your options. Do you want to upgrade your present degree? What learning options are available to you? Explore some of the available opportunities such as adult education, distance learning, online learning, home study. What about financing options? What's available to you?

Have a plan. What steps can I take? Make a plan to achieve your education or training goal. Where can you begin? Perhaps it's by calling your local college to request a catalog. Explore the Internet for online learning opportunities. Develop a step-by-step plan to move your toward your educational goals.

MAINTAINING A POSITIVE ATTITUDE

Let's face it. Nobody wants to be around negative people except other negative people. Your attitude is a choice. You can choose to be positive or you can choose to be a grumpy, complaining individual. Personally, I'd rather be positive and feel good.

A simple way to maintain this positive attitude is to read or listen to uplifting tapes daily. If you invest just ten minutes a day in reading inspirational, uplifting books or listening to tapes, you will find yourself feeling and acting better than before. If you doubt this, give it a try for just thirty days.

RESPONSIBILITY

In today's business environment, too many people are looking for where to place the blame for everything that goes wrong. Leaders take responsibility. Former president, Harry Truman is known for the statement, "The buck stops here." If you want to be a true leader, learn to take responsibility for your actions and results. If you make a mistake, so be it.

Leaders are not without mistakes, however, they learn from them and become better for it. Follow through on what you say you'll do. This one simple act can put you above the crowd since most people are poor about following through on their actions. If you tell someone you will call them next week, do it! If you say you will send an article to a person, follow through. You'll be amazed at how much people appreciate this.

ADAPTABILITY

If you want to thrive rather than just survive, you'll want to develop a positive attitude toward change and a respect for diversity. Our work culture is changing radically. If we are to be happy, we must learn to adapt to these changes.

CULTIVATE YOUR TEAM-BUILDING SKILLS

Companies want team players. In order to excel in the workplace, you'll want to cultivate your team-building skills. While there are many good team-building books and training programs, below are some tips to get you started. If you want to learn more, seek out the material that you need. Below are some of the skills you'll need to develop in order to work well with others and achieve the optimum results:

- Be a team player.
- Contribute to the organization's goals.
- Work within the culture of the group.
- Plan and make decisions with others and support their

viewpoints and objectives.

- Respect the opinions of others in the group.
- Exercise "give and take" to achieve group results.
- Seek a team approach as appropriate.
- Lead when appropriate, mobilizing the team for high performance.

RISING ABOVE THE PACK

To get promoted, you need to rise above the pack. You need to stand out and get noticed. Here are some ways to help you enhance your appraisals:

- Help solve important problems. Consider doing extra work or research on your own time.

- Get published. Write a piece that will put your organization in a good light, or show your knowledge of your field. It could be in a trade or professional association publication, or in your own company's newsletter.

- Develop your speaking skills. A great way to do this is to join Toastmasters International. Look in your local telephone directory for the location nearest you or go to their web site at www.toastmasters.org.

- Network with people beyond your own team or department. Offer to help team members and co-workers, but keep your own work the top priority.

- Keep your resumé current. Ask someone influential about where to send it within your company. Let a few select people see that you're serious about career advancement.

- Do good work and make sure it gets noticed.

WHEN CHANGE IS INEVITABLE

Sometimes it becomes necessary to find a new job in order to be happy. If this is your situation, there are some things you can do to make the process more effective and increase the possibility you'll find the work you want. Once you have completed the exercises in this book and spent some time reflecting about what you really want from your work, you're ready to take a proactive approach to finding the ideal job. There are several things that will assist you in this process — your networking skills, your resumé and your interviewing skills.

NETWORKING FOR YOUR IDEAL WORK

One of the best ways to find your ideal work is to spread the word throughout your personal network. Your friends, associates and colleagues are some of the best sources for employment information. In today's tight job market, companies are even offering bonuses to employees who help them recruit people. Many of the best jobs available never make it to the classified section. They are filled through networking. This is especially true of top management positions.

Think about who you know. Who might they know? Make a list of your family, friends, associates, co-workers, casual acquaintances and everyone else you can think of. Prioritize your list by who knows you best and by who may be in the best position to help. Your aunt Jo, having worked as a bookkeeper for thirty years in a company may be in a much better position than your friend who just started his job. Her opinion is probably highly regarded and her suggestion better received.

ASK, ASK, ASK AND THEN ASK SOME MORE

Don't be afraid to ask for help. It's human nature to want to help each other. If you're a good worker and I refer you to my company and they are thrilled with having you work there, everyone wins — including me.

When you're speaking to people about how you'd like them to help you, be specific. If you want them to open a door for you, say so. Avoid saying things like, "Well, Tom, if you hear of anything, please let me know." Instead, be direct. You might say something like, "Tom, I'm looking for a new position. Is there someone in your acquaintance you can recommend I speak with?" If the person is a close associate or friend, ask if you can use his or her name as a referral. If they're a good friend, they may even be able to make an introductory call for you.

KNOW WHAT YOU WANT

When you ask people for help, don't expect them to figure out what you do or what you're looking for. Tell them your experience or the kind of work you're looking for. If you've been a computer operator for years but want to change into sales, let them know. Very often people's understanding of what we do is very far from reality, even people who are close to us. When was the last time your family understood what you really do at work all day? If you're like most of us, their impression is way off target so, if you expect them to help, you have to make sure they have the right details. You could even give them a one-page snapshot of your accomplishments and career goals as an aid to help them better understand what you want.

Six degrees of separation

Remember the idea of "six degrees of separation" which reminds us that any person is within six people (or degrees) of any other person. Think about this. Someone you know is six people away from anyone else you may want to meet. If there is a particular person you want to meet or a company you're interested in, someone you know can start the ball rolling. It starts with you asking for what you need and then being willing to accept the help when it's offered.

Your responsibility

If you're asking someone to help you, be sure to follow through on their assistance. There's nothing worse than taking the time to open a door for another person only to find out that they never made the call. The person trying to help you will feel foolish and will probably be less than anxious to help again. Also, be sure to send a little thank-you note to people when they've been a help. A little gift is not out of the ordinary and will show others you appreciate their efforts. People are busy and if you're asking them to do you a favor, your responsibility is to at least acknowledge their efforts.

RESUMÉS—YOUR PERSONAL SALES TOOL

Your resumé is your sales tool. It is often the only means someone has of determining whether or not you are qualified for a particular assignment. It is your primary spokesperson. Be sure your resumé indicates not only your job responsibilities but your accomplishments as well. Your resumé is your own private sales-person and should easily communicate your personal strengths.

To begin, don't write your resumé. Just take time to list out everything you have accomplished. Accomplishments are not job description terms but are results. Results are things that highlight you and sell you. They can include contributions, financial changes, programs you developed, skills you brought to the job, new ideas you gave the organization, targets you hit, sales you generated, etc. The goal of the resumé is to get you an interview. To get in the door for the interview you are going to have to get the reader to see why they need you and this is because of your accomplishments not because of your job description. See the difference?

In formatting the job description, remember to include a vision or objective. This should highlight the type of position you want to fill and should match what you may already know the company is looking for. Using a computer, you can easily customize your objectives to match the job you're applying for. By tailoring each resumé submission to the particular job, you'll make a better impression and increase the likelihood of your being granted an interview.

Next, provide an executive summary. This is where you highlight those talents and skills to show who you are and what you will bring to the company. Use bullet form here.

Now, list your professional experience. Again, results should be stated. Education follows with degrees listed if they support your job objective. Finally, include any professional associations. Do not say, "references will be provided upon request" or make any comment regarding references. If they ask for them, of course you will provide them.

Finally, double and triple-check spelling and grammar. You need to make a great impression. Use high quality paper and matching envelopes for your resumé. Don't forget this is your brochure, so spend money on it and make it a powerful sales tool of your achievements.

WINNING THE INTERVIEW

John F. Kennedy, in his classic speech said, "Ask not what your country can do for you, ask what you can do for your country." This was good advice for Americans and it's good advice for anyone going on a job interview. Too many people make the mistake of giving the impression that they're only concerned with themselves. While your needs are of the utmost importance to you, as an interviewer, I want to know what you're going to do for the company first. Then we'll get to what the company will do for you.

The job interview is your opportunity to sell yourself to the prospective employer. It is your chance and, perhaps, your only chance to convince them you are the perfect person for the job. How, then, can you insure your success? While there are no guarantees, a few preparations will go a long way toward your getting the position.

Be prepared

That's not only good advice for Boy Scouts, it's good for you, too. The better prepared you are, the better your chance of making a good first impression.

Before the interview

Before going on any job interview, research the company you're interviewing with and their industry. The easiest way to do this is to go to the company's web-site. There you'll probably find all the information you could ever want about your prospective employer. While you're online, check out other companies in the same industry. The more intelligently you can speak about their business, the better your chance of getting the job.

Practice the interview with a friend or family member. Let them ask you pointed interview questions and have them question your qualifications. Practice in front of a mirror. Plan what you want to say about yourself. Know your goals and outcomes. Affirm that you are good at interviewing. Even if you don't fully believe it, it's better than affirming that you're a poor interviewee.

Visualize the interview. Imagine you're at the interview. Sit quietly and run through the interviewing process in your mind. Imagine yourself sitting with the interviewer, answering his or her questions. See yourself poised, relaxed and confident. In your mind's eye, see the interviewing going wonderfully for you. See yourself and the interviewer smiling and having a great talk. See yourself standing at the end of the interview, smiling and shaking hands. Let yourself feel the feelings of a terrific interview. This technique has been used successfully by some of the top people in the selling profession as well as professional athletes. Use the power of your mind to help you succeed.

Keep a positive attitude. The Harvard Business Review reports that eighty-five percent of the reason most people obtain and keep a job is attitude, while aptitude is only fifteen percent. Skills can always be taught and most employers would rather teach a person with a winning attitude the necessary skills than the other way around.

DURING THE INTERVIEW

During the actual interview, you will feel relaxed, knowing you're well-prepared. Dress your best. A sure sign of a healthy self-esteem is someone who dresses their best at all times. This does not have to mean expensive but does mean you should look the part. If you're going for a management job, a suit and tie for men and suit or dress for women is appropriate. If, on the other hand, you're applying for a position as an automobile mechanic, a more casual approach may be appropriate. Match your wardrobe to the position as much as possible. Always tell the truth. If you're unsure of an answer, say so. No one expects you to know everything but they do expect you to admit what you don't know. Emphasize your strengths and downplay your weaknesses.

Leave money until the last part of the interview. If you really want a position and a company really wants you, financial agreements are a lot easier. Of course, you should have an idea of the salary before going on the interview. Every job has industry standards and companies know it.

EVERYONE'S FAVORITE INTERVIEW QUESTION

I can almost guarantee you the interviewer will say, "Tell me about yourself." A friend of mine would always ask this question of new salespeople he was interviewing. He felt that if they could not handle this simple communication, they would probably not be well-suited for a sales position.

If the person hesitated and started saying things like, "Um ... well ... I ah ..." and so on, he knew they'd never make it in sales.

When you are asked this question, and you will be, it is a great time for you to communicate your strengths. When asked to tell the interviewer about yourself, you might say, "I am a well-educated woman, with a strong work ethic. I like challenge and growth and feel I am an asset to any company." This is more likely to get you the job than stumbling. Rehearse your answer to this question until it no longer sounds rehearsed. Be sincere but be self-assured. People want to hire people who have a healthy self-image.

AFTER THE INTERVIEW

Take the time to send a thank-you letter. This accomplishes two things. It is a courtesy to the interviewer and it gives you the opportunity to restate the reasons they should hire you. Remind the interviewer of your qualifications (briefly) and give them a way to contact you. If for some reason you decide to decline the offer, thank them anyway. You don't want to burn any bridges. People have a way of moving around the job scene and you never know who may be a great contact in the future.

CONCLUSION

*N*ow, you're on your own. The time has come for you to take whatever action you feel is necessary. Do you want a new job? What about a totally new career? Has the time come for you to start your own business? Perhaps you've learned you really like your present company and want to advance within your organization. Whatever your desire, now is the time to begin moving toward working yourself happy.

I have tried to give you ideas, tools and some insight into what's available to you in your career. Now you must act, however, you need not do it alone. You may want to engage the services of a professional coach.

To learn more about the field of coaching, visit our web site at http://www.comprehensivecoaching.com.

You may want to look for a career support group in your area or even on the Internet. Many of the job search boards have message boards where you can discuss what's on your mind.

As you *Work Yourself Happy*, I offer you the time and space to enjoy the process and the journey. I thank you for allowing me to begin coaching you to see the world of possibilities brought to you in this book.

TAKE THE CHALLENGE

Email your story and tell us how you've used the ideas in this book to work yourself happy. With your permission, your article may become part of our virtual WYH community on the Internet and you may even be in the next edition of *Work Yourself Happy*. Email to story@comprehensivecoaching.com to share your success with other readers.

FREE NEWSLETTER

To subscribe to my *free* email newsletter, visit www.comprehensivecoaching.com and click on the newsletter link for Coaches Corner.

INDIVIDUAL AND GROUP SERVICES

Individual and Group Coaching, Business Consulting, Motivational *Work Yourself Happy* and other workshops and presentations, keynote speeches.

www.comprehensivecoaching.com

PROFESSIONAL COACH TRAINING

Customized Training, Coach Training for Professionals, Coaching programs to be more effective in your current profession or for learning to become a coach.

www.comprehensivecoachingu.com

DISTRIBUTOR INQUIRES AND BULK ORDERS

For bulk orders or wholesale distribution, please call (215) 699-4949 or Email bookfulfillment@aol.com.

Whatever path you choose, you owe it to yourself to

Work Yourself Happy

ABOUT THE AUTHOR

Terri Levine's coaching clients call her the *Wisdom Wizard* — and for good reason. As an entrepreneur, she owned her own speech therapy practice and quickly went on to compile an impressive track record of growing million dollar businesses as her career expanded. As a sales and marketing professional, Terri quickly rose to become number one in national sales. As an executive within the rehabilitation industry, she created one astounding success after another, including the development of a $22 million dollar revenue base in a three-year time span.

She then left behind her position as regional president of a healthcare corporation to begin coaching others to discover their own joy from finding the work that was in their hearts. Terri loves conducting *Work Yourself Happy* workshops and training seminars for companies and organizations. Terri used what she learned as she worked herself from speech-language pathologist, to business owner, to art consultant, to hospital administrator, to marketing director, to regional president — only to find that she was not enjoying her work. Terri re-invented her career and her life and is skilled at assisting clients to find their passion, and create a life and career that is joyful. She believes work can be a natural extension of your true self and she looks forward to each day's work — a far cry from her previous experiences.

She is a professional coach, consultant and founder of *Comprehensive Coaching U,* The Coach Training Program for Professionals. Terri writes several e-zines each week, which are distributed to an international audience. She has published many articles on coaching, management, leadership and career transition. She is a highly-sought-after speaker and trainer and is known for her exciting, interactive, professional and powerful presentations.

She is a graduate of Comprehensive Coaching U and Coach U. She received her Master of Science from Ithaca College, and her Bachelor's from the University of Pittsburgh. Terri is an active member of the International Coach Federation and is also a member of the National Association of Women Business Owners, the American Society of Training and Development, a charter member of the Philadelphia Area Coaches Alliance, a member of Business Network International and the American Speech-Language-Hearing Association.

As a coach, Terri listens deeply to her clients and becomes their partner in discovering better ways to grow profitable businesses, restore balance in their lives, and bring greater joy to each day. Terri coaches a variety of clients ranging from CEOs to small business owners and professionals.

Terri loves her work. Her dream is to see others enjoying each work-day the way she does. She lives in Montgomery County, PA, with her husband, Mark, her father, Walter, and her dog, Sheba.